STRONG
I AM

A unique perspective on Love, Self Esteem,
Money and many more essentials.

Dale Vidal

Published 2016 by

Guava Gap Publishing LLC
P.O. Box 590481
Ft Lauderdale, FL 33359
Website: www.guavagap.com
Email: guavagap@outlook.com

ISBN: 0997382503
ISBN 978-0-9973825-0-1

Printed in the United States of America

TABLE OF CONTENTS

INTRODUCTION

Who can say for certain what tomorrow will be like? At best, we make solid plans today for tomorrow's possibilities. A significant part of that preparation process is self-help. Self- help is one's ability to help self.

Strong I Am is a collective work which covers a 7 year period. These affirmations provide you with the tools needed to adapt to changing circumstances. No two journeys are identical but there are similarities. *Strong I Am* gives you a unique and valuable perspective on challenges and how to overcome them. **Strong I Am.**

CHAPTER 1

LIGHT OF MINE

I have something inside of me
It always wants everything to work out well
It loves to do what is right and it is always looking for itself in other people
This thing inside of me is exciting and free
It is disciplined and intelligent too
It knows itself very well and it is not pleased with anyone who tries to hurt it in anyway
This thing inside of me defends itself by speaking the truth
All that is true is it and it is all true
Whenever it finds itself in others it tries to learn from them and it teaches them too
It is not in every person
Those who have it, cherishes it and are attentive to it

Those who do not have it are locked away in a place they call *misery*
The people in *misery* are always telling lies
They are always accusing other people and their accusations are always wrong.
Of course, this is no surprise because these people are blinded by the lies inside of them
This thing inside of me knows all these things and so it chooses its friends wisely
Friends make this thing inside of me rejoice and whenever I rejoice I laugh
Friends point out all my strengths and they encourage me to exercise my strengths so my strengths will become stronger
Friends help me in a positive way; they help me to look at my weaknesses.
When I look at my weaknesses, I can examine them.
Then I think of things that I can do to turn my weaknesses into strengths.
For example, I do not know how to swim. Swimming is a survival skill.
Not knowing how to swim is a weakness.
I pay for and attend to swimming lessons.
Now I know how to swim. I have a lifetime skill. I can swim
Thanks to this thing inside of me and my friends!

CHAPTER 2
RESPONSIBILITY

I think the people around me are taking me for granted. Whenever they need me, they call me and I rush right over. It's been that way for years. They use to say "thank you", but now, they get upset if I don't rush over when they call. I love these people. I want to be there for them in every possible way. Still, I'm starting to think that rushing over every time they call is not the best thing for them.

"Oh, I'm sorry to hear that. So what are you going to do about it?" Yes, this will be my approach the next time they call. It's not that I've stopped caring. I'm just caring in a different way. I don't think that you can love someone too much; but I do feel that there are effective ways of loving someone as well as ineffective ways of loving someone. For example, over feeding a fish can cause severe discomfort for the fish. Over feeding the fish can also be fatal. On the other hand, if I research the fish eating habits and I follow feeding guidelines, then we can share a long and healthy relationship. Every morning the sun rises and at noon the heat from the sun is optimum. In the evening, the sun rests and the moon rises. This dance between the sun and the moon creates a balance. Balance is essential in everything we do. Wanting to be there for the ones I love is a natural and healthy propensity. Rushing over to put out the fire each and every time they call is ineffective and unhealthy. This behavior could be compared to over feeding the fish.

With every challenge, there is an opportunity to grow. Growth requires taking personal responsibility for our actions or inactions. Owning the responsibility then allows us to understand the challenge and master it. I think I've been taking the people around me for granted.

CHAPTER 3

LOVE

Love is the truth that brings people together. Once people are together they usually create bonds. There are casual bonds, intimate bonds, and professional bonds. Regardless of the type of bond that is formed, love is what keeps that bond together.

When two people are in love with each other, they do everything together. This is not to say that they are always together but their going and coming amounts to one goal. When they look at each other, they see a friend. Their actions or deeds toward each other are friendly. Love is extraordinary because it is honest. Sometimes love will say "I understand how you're feeling but that was not love, that was lust." Another time love will say "take it slow, let's do some observations." When love is satisfied with itself, it says "You have me. Where do you want to go? I'll go with you." Love always loves.

CHAPTER 4
TASK

As long as you're doing something positive, no one can harm you. The positive that you do is you. You are doing you. A task has 5 parts: what, when, where, why and how.

Everything that we do is a task. Anything that you start you must finish. It is improper to start something and leave it undone. All distractions ask the same question, "Are you serious about what you're doing?" If you are serious, you will learn to turn any distraction into a motivational tool. A distraction is really a reminder to stay focus on what you are doing. Glory is in the beginning, the middle builds character and to finish is to be victorious.

CHAPTER 5

DIRTY DOUBT

At this moment I will start to believe in myself and in the near future I will do all the things I now dream of doing.

There is this stranger they call him 'dirty doubt'. Whenever time I try to do something, dirty doubt tries to stop me. He mostly talks to me in my mind but sometimes he speaks through other people too. Dirty doubt is always saying "I can't" or "You can't". The old people told me that dirty doubt always wants to receive but he never ever wants to give. He sits around all day with nothing positive to do and so he tries to get others to sit around with him doing absolutely nothing positive. His home is dirty and his kitchen is filled with urine and feces. This is why they call him dirty doubt. Dirty doubt has a brother; they

call him 'dirty fear'. Dirty fear only wants to trick
me but I won't let him trick me. He always wants me
to think about things that are not real. Why should
I be afraid when I can pray? From this moment on
I will stop listening to dirty doubt and his brother
dirty fear.

CHAPTER 6
STONES

Look at it for what it is
Sometimes we have a hard time doing this
People will say yes when they really mean no
One thing is for sure though
Survival is King
Food Water Clothing Shelter
Thank you for calling
How may I help you?
If you have ever been to the river, you know that at the river, there are small stones, big stones and even bigger stones.
Sometimes we use the small stones as stepping stones to the bigger stones
Love is the only thing that lasts forever lasting everything else is circumstantial

Dale Vidal

I'm always loving myself
Whenever I plan, I'm loving myself
If you should see me thinking, I'm loving myself
I just have to make it to the top of the bigger stones.

CHAPTER 7

A WOMAN STORY

Time is the measurement of possibility
A woman loves time as long as it is giving and not taking
If it is taking she becomes jealous of it
Yesterday she loved it. Today she resents it and will set out to destroy it
Any means necessary.
A good woman is simple
A complicated woman is a thorn to any fool
If you should see a complicated woman strolling down the street
Run in the opposite direction
She is like the wind, her coordinates are unsearchable
Leave her alone.
A woman has needs
Seven minutes ago she needed to be heard

Three minutes ago she needed to be hugged
This very moment she needs to be caressed tenderly
Three minutes from now she will need to hear sweet
whispers in her ears
Seven minutes from now she will need to be gamed
Nine hours from now she will need to be left alone
to reminisce and recuperate.
Each time a woman cries, a part of her slips away
into a place call 'the reservoir'
The reservoir is a storage area in the woman's psyche
This area stores her most precious asset, -her
innocence
This is where all the cards are placed on the table
No dealing allowed
The weak has no place here
They are outside the gate nursing their wounds with
fancy lines and expensive bribes
Only a King may enter into the Queen's chamber
and uncover the mystery of a woman
Truth
A Woman Story

CHAPTER 8
INTIMACY

First come friendship, then intimacy. Intimacy is trusting. People who forego friendship do not get intimacy. They get sex. Sex is 100% physical and 0% spiritual. Intimacy is spiritual. Intimacy brings healthy children. Sometimes our past experiences make us afraid of intimacy. Remember, intimacy is what makes the difference between what is truth-full and what is not. You feel truth all the time and that feeling is life. Lies only use people. Lying is usury Burn usury, usury going nowhere wherein it is no. Children must feel safe all the time. A friend is someone who makes you feel good, makes you laugh. A friend encourages you to stay positive. Good, Better, Best. Loyalty shines the brightest among friends. A touch is a gesture asking for more intimacy. The senses are keenest in intimacy. Have you ever seen a color that made you feel good? Yes, colors do affect the way we feel. I love a woman who smells good. I love a woman who is confident. I want our confidence to be a part of our children.

CHAPTER 9

A FATHER

I have heard many different voices in my life. A father's voice is not the loudest and it is not the softest. A father's voice is.

Imagine you are walking in the forest. Whenever you are unsure about which path to take, a father's voice is there to guide you. A father is not perfect. He has made some mistakes himself. He learns from his life experiences and he makes better choices with each passing day. He sees himself in his children.

No one knows what tomorrow will be like in exact. Each and every one knows this moment. Fatherhood and Motherhood is sacred. It's serious and it's fun.

A father who is alive and is absent from his children, is missing a core part of his potential. He will never be completely satisfied with himself. Father,

Mother and Children represent a unit known as the heritage. Heritage is where endurance lives. Fathers, let us continue to endure.

CHAPTER 10
FASHION

I am romantic. Lilies and rose petals floating on top of the water. Purple silk, red silk, yellow silk, adorning the mahogany wood. You feel me when I walk in the room. I am calm. I am effortless. You just love to look at me. Green is not a romantic color. Kisko colors, Cherry O'Baby. Cashmere feels nice on the skin. Cashmere is perfect in the fall season. Orange cashmere is playful, red is executively romantic, pink is comely. Dinner on cruises and home entertainment such as satin parties (singles only). Yellow is safe.

Satin is a contact fabric. In other words, satin is seductive, it makes you want to touch it. Satin and pearls is a nice combination. When a woman wears a blouse, buttoned up with pearls tucked inside, she is saying "take your time, I'm not going anywhere."

I am casual just like food or the air you breathe. I make you comfortable. My approach is indirect. I'm easy to work with because I am casual. I have the most color variation imaginable. In the heat of summer I am cool. It's the colors, white, yellow, sky blue. Light colors for the summer. Sweating in clothes is so uncool. So it's important to always observe the weather. Fall means that the temperature is falling, so then the colors change. They become a little darker. The color decides how much heat I will retain. Corduroy is great when the temperature is in the mid to high 60's and low 70's.

CHAPTER 11
HARD TIMES

I am running out of money. I am running out of food. No one is hiring, what will I do? My family have done all that they could. My enemies have done all that they could. I hear some people shouting; they're telling me to stay on my feet. I hear some people jeering; they're hoping to see me fall. I cannot fall. I will not fall.

Throughout my adult life, I have been an hourly worker. Working for the greatest companies in the world until they no longer needed my labor. It seems as if I'm caught up in a cycle. They say "You're the best, you're the greatest worker." A couple years later, here comes the pink colored paper. Somehow I have to break away from this cycle. Many years have passed; I'm not getting any younger. How do

I start? Who do I see? I have no stocks. I have no shareholders.

It was at that moment I heard a voice saying "Hello young man and welcome to your Initial Public Offering. I am the voice of Reason and I am here to answer your three questions." I wasn't afraid. The voice of Reason sounded familiar and so I listened intently to what he had to offer. He said to me, "Young man, what talent do you have? What joy have you garnered?" I replied "I always had a way with words, the Alpha, the Beths, always a pleasure to write, to share, to reckon, to care." With three breaths of Reason, I was taken from the mouth of despair. Reason said "You will continue to write, you will continue to share, you will meet many, your talent is your pay."

CHAPTER 12
ORIGINATORS

Yes, it's easy to do that same thing in that same way as everyone else. The popular way usually has a very predictable outcome. The 1st person to ever do it usually benefits the most. He or She was the originator of doing it that way. That way is now popular because most people want to do that same thing in that same way. But those people will never be the originator; they will always be the followers. A concept or an idea is original once and then everything else is a copy. People may improve the original idea but that improvement is a follow up. How do originators do what they do?

The first step is to step away from the popular crowd. Popular people are not risk takers. In their mind they have it good, they're popular. They say "why take risks that may ruin a good thing?" Popular people always play it safe. An originator knows that leadership is inherently risky. Leadership is fore-knowledge in motion. Nothing is guaranteed, but 1+1 always equal 2. Originators make moves. These moves are regulated by calculations. Calculations come from first hand observations of actions and re-actions. It is glorious to be the first at something that benefit billions of people.

The journey to glory is not easy. The people closest to you may turn on you. They may have been there when you first started, but as you go further up the hill their eyes can only see the difficulties. Always remember that you are the originator. Even though you can see the bright morning star in the darkest abyss, others won't be able to see it. You just have to keep on moving towards that star. When you touch it, then you will be the light that shines everywhere. People will see your glory and they will want to be like you. These people are called 'popular people'. They only see the light shining but they do not know the journey to that light. You the originator must remember 2 important things. First, you must patent or copyright your contribution to humanity. This protection will ensure that your children, your grandchildren and your great grandchildren will inherit wealth. Originators who patent their valuable inventions are wealthy. Popular people who copy originators may get rich. Wealth is superior to riches. The second thing to remember is the journey. You must remember how you got to that 1st star. We're not the type to sit around chatting over tea. Before they know it, we're on our way to the next morning star.

CHAPTER 13

MANEUVERING

This is a discussion on maneuvering through swamp land. A swamp is defined as 'a wet spongy land, saturated and sometimes partially or intermittently covered with water.'[1]

In the swamp, one must not place too much emphasis on speed. It is better to pace yourself. If you choose to speed, you may miss something, like a 12 foot crocodile in wait or a brand new power engine boat swaying in the marshes. Getting out of the swamp and unto higher ground should be your aim. Stopping here and there to mingle is like a bird that has wandered from its nest. It is dangerous and this wasteful delay may be fatal. Therefore, the warrior keeps his focus and prevents himself from being distracted.

If you have been in a swamp for most of your life and it is your heart's desire to get out, you must first be thankful that you're alive; next you must equip yourself to make an escape.

Some people like it when the swamp is full. Sometimes these people walk on others and sometimes they run on others. They do this when they are moving from one side of the swamp to the other side. To prevent them from stepping on you, align yourself with thorns. Then, if they should step on you they will find themselves in excruciating pain. They will then fall into the swamp and be eaten by that crocodile.

Drinking alcohol will only make you want to party. Partying in the swamp is like partying in hell. The devil and his associates have you surrounded and you are drunk and exhausted. Avoid nightclubs, sex shops and bars. There are some who have deceived themselves into liking the swamp. These are the murderers, the robbers and those who lust for married women. They are boastful in poverty, rowdy in ignorance and cunning in foolishness. At this very moment they are sinking in quick sand. So, how do you get out of the swamp? Take off the extra baggage and throw it a distance away from your feet. Fix your eyes on higher ground and move towards it.

'Webster's II New Riverside Dictionary, 1984.

CHAPTER 14
CHARACTER

King Solomon said "Praise for a fool is out of place, like snow in summer or rain at harvest time." According to the United Nation Population Fund, there are over 7 billion people on the earth.[1] Each person on earth is an individual. Identical twins are very similar physically and to a large extent emotionally as well. However, there is always something distinctive between the twins. There is always something that sets the identical twins apart from each other. The most prominent indicator of an individual is what is called *character*. Character is genetic. Every new born baby has predispositions. These predispositions are the root of the child's personality and they are inherited from the parents. A comedian's character is happy and caring.

A businessperson's character is shrewd and attentive. An adventurer's character is curious. Character makes the person.

I am a builder. I like to build things. When I was about 9 years old, my parents gave me a dog. I was responsible for feeding, grooming and cleaning up after the dog. Over the years, we grew together and that experience taught me how to care for someone else other than myself.

At age 22, I had graduated from college. I had also built a successful economic structure and I was always looking for people to care for. There was one thing that I had not yet learnt. *A builder must be in the company of other builders.* Per adventure a builder finds himself in the company of destroyers. Then whatever that builder builds, his companions will destroy.

Once you've identified your character, take the time to develop it. On your way to perfection, you will need to network with others who are on the same path as you. You will know them by the things they say and the things they do. Birds fly with other birds that look like them, behave like them and eat the same food as them. Some people's character is deception. These people never do what they say. This is how you'll know them. *Be careful about who you care for.*

Your experience is your road map to realizing your full potential. Your character is your passport to wherever you want to go. A good character cannot be bought. It's never available on the market for sale or trade. I am a builder and I am proud of it.

[1] United Nation Population Fund, Oct 2011.

CHAPTER 15

MONEY

I don't like money. If I could survive without it, I would banish it from my presence. It's too bossy. I've tried leaving it alone but money won't leave me alone. Whenever I have a lot of money, the people around me behave like puppets. If I say yes they say yes. If I say no they say no. No matter what I do, they won't tell me how they feel. I have a lot of money. Still, I feel lonely in a room full of people.

Whenever I don't have any money, people look at me funny. I can't get them to agree with anything I say. It's like a circus. If I say yes they say no. If I say no they say yes. Once people realize that I have no money, they become suspicious. It's crazy but it's true. I don't need money, but I do need food, clothing and shelter. It turns out that the grocery stores have to pay their workers, so they can't give me the food for free. The department stores have to pay their workers too, so they need me to pay them money for the clothes. I can just see the landlord now. He's a nervous wreck. He has a mortgage to pay. He has property tax to pay. If I don't have any money to pay the landlord, he'll probably have a nervous breakdown. But not before he kicks me off his property. Now I am homeless, naked and hungry.

I know what you're thinking. Money has me in a corner, right? For now, yeah, but I figured out money. Having no money is a waste of time, because you can't do anything without money. You may have the greatest ideas in the world. People don't listen unless money is involved. I still don't like money. Money is too bossy. I will tolerate money for now.

I love to work. I will work hard and earn a lot of money and then I will buy a farm. I'll work the farm and grow my own food. I'll learn to make my own clothes. I'll live on the farm. So there it is; food, clothing and shelter requirement is met.

People who behave like puppets don't like to work. Everyone around me will work the farm. Physical labor brings out the best and the worst in people. When you're bending, standing and then bending under the pelting hot sun, playing puppet is the last thing on your mind. I think I'll keep money around. Money is a good defence.

CHAPTER 16
DIVORCE

The statistics say that at least 50% of all marriages end in divorce. I was once married and now I am divorced. This is my opinion on divorce. A divorce is mostly emotional. Anger is the dominant emotion in a divorce. When a person is angry, it is difficult for that person to listen. Listening is the first step in solving any problem. The mind has to receive information, examine it and then respond to it. However, when a person feels betrayed by a love one, they sometimes become fearful. Fear is a dangerous emotion. Instead of researching the unknown, fear causes its victim to avoid the unknown. This is why people who are angry and fearful are unwilling to listen to new thoughts and ideas. The only people who are listening are the attorneys. The attorneys are listening for the fear, the anger and the types of asset that the couple may have.

Divorce offers one benefit to society. A divorce legally separates two people who are usually irrational and angry at that particular time. There are no winners in a divorce, except for the attorneys of course. If you are married, your husband or your wife is your primary priority. If your friends or your relatives are not supportive of your spouse then by default they become a distraction and they should be treated as such. This does not include marriages where domestic violence is occurring. Domestic violence is a crime and immediate professional intervention is necessary.

Even though at least 50% of all marriages end in a divorce, some couples grow old together. There is an old saying *"Take time to know the one you love."* When you know a person well, you will always know the best approach. The best approach will get you the best results 100% of the time. The wrong approach will only start fires here, there and everywhere. Who really wants to be putting out fires when they could be making love?

Some people are fortunate enough to be forewarned. Some people are mature enough to learn from their past experience. But what all people have in common is a choice. I choose to listen.

CHAPTER 17

LONELINESS

Loneliness, there was a time when I needed you, because everything that I thought was true was really false and all that I thought was false turned out to be true. I was confused.

There were many nights when we reminisced together you and I.

You were the rock that I stood on when everything around me was sinking.

You taught me that silence is pure and that truth never compromise. Now the earth's fury is calm and the down is up.

Loneliness, are we meant to be together forever?

I feel our alliance is circumstantial.

Late at nights I toss and turn in my bed. On the weekends, I find myself at the beach admiring the beautiful women. I'm at the library studying the beautiful women. Instead of driving my car, I'm riding my bicycle for miles at a time, just so I can hear the sounds of the street.

No one wants to be lonely but sometimes we need to be alone.

Loneliness is a refuge, it is not a home.

CHAPTER 18

POVERTY

Poverty is a crime planned by twisted rich people against the poor. These rich people say "If we can keep them poor then we can rule over them." They say "We the rich control the circulation of money. We give you money after you have labored and you give it right back in exchange for our bills." They continue by saying "We the rich sit amongst ourselves and we plan our future. We the rich also plan the future of the poor." This is what the rich says.

The poor man hopes. The poor man hopes that one day he will control his own destiny. The poor man hopes that one day he will live his dreams. The poor man goes to bed hungry sometimes. When the poor man salivates and belly pain sets in, he has no food to turn away the hunger. The poor man is a victim of poverty.

The twisted rich people say "Our studies show that once the poor man is hungry he will eventually break down and begin to steal. Look see! They're stealing from each other." The rich says "Let's give a few of them some guns. They'll use the guns to kill each other. Look see! They're killing each other."

There are intellectual communities who are hired by twisted rich people. As they all raise their champagne filled glasses, the intellects say, "Our studies are conclusive. Write us another check for a couple more millions and we'll continue to monitor our studies." Poverty is a crime planned by twisted rich people against the poor.

CHAPTER 19
SELF ESTEEM

I look at the world and the people in the world from the **inside out**. My value system is 100% internal. My self-worth comes from me. Out of 1000 advisers, I may listen to 1. Out of 10,000 advisers, I may listen to 10. I don't know everything but I do know how to feel, how to smell, how to taste, how to look and how to listen.

Low self-esteem occurs when a person looks at the world from the **outside in**. A person who suffers from low self-esteem is not aware of his or her self-worth. This disconnection from self causes the person to rely on others to give him or her a self-worth.

If I am walking down the street and someone says to me "Dale, you are ugly". I would respond by saying "that's your opinion and also your loss." I know it to be a fact that I am handsome. I've never seen anyone who looked exactly like me. That makes me handsome and unique. A fact is information that has been verified. An opinion is speculative and opinions have a tendency to change like the weather.

Let's say that I continued walking down that street and someone else says to me "Dale, you are the greatest." I would reply by saying "Thank You" Within myself, I know that I am not the greatest. I am one of the greats but I am not the greatest. My creator is the greatest. Still, it always feels good to know that someone else sees that greatness in me.

Others may be able to see my potential but I am my potential. My confidence goes hand in hand with my self-esteem. Trying new things that require hard work on my part is a great tool for building up my confidence. The more effort I put into my new project the more progress I will see. Since I am careful about who I take advise from, it is important that I am honest with myself. If I am terrible at basketball then I won't tell myself that I am a great basketball player. Instead, I would learn the skills associated with basketball by observing others and practicing. My dribble may be awkward looking at first. My shots may be scandalously off target but I'm learning. It's true; practice makes for a great dribble and a beautiful jump shot.

CHAPTER 20
EFFICIENCY

On your mark, Get set, Go. From Point A to Point Z with the least amount of waste.

Is it not written that each man has a purpose in his lifetime? Furthermore, is it not also written that his task is to identify his purpose and then work towards fulfilling that purpose?

On the grand outlook and inlook of things, wouldn't it be better to know love than to know grief and despair? Nothing feels as good as a smile. There are some people living in this world who have not had any good news in a long while. We're talking decades here. This is the life of the oppressed. How much does it cost to speak the truth? What is the stock market's index price on caring?

I make sure my family, friends and all members of the Love community know how much they mean to me. You are the greatest! Keep being who you are. Love is the answer.

CHAPTER 21

THE FUTURE

The future is now. This moment is the future. Tomorrow is not guaranteed. This moment in time is guaranteed. Place your palm over your heart. Feel your heart beat. Your heartbeat is the rhythm of your here and now. Nothing is realer than the heartbeat.

People ask me "What do you want to do in the future?" and I reply "I am doing the future right now." Here's how it works. In my mind, I can see myself at my ultimate or my peak. My here and now is a build-up to my ultimate. Everything I do while I am awake is a prelude to my ultimate. My future is now. I think about my ultimate every day and every night. I know that I have to rest and I know that I have to work. I do not cheat my rest and I do not cheat my work. I live in the future. I do my best to satisfy all my heart's desires. If I don't fulfill my heart's desires, then they will not be fulfilled. The language that I speak is very old. It is the first language that was ever spoken. I speak love. Love is simple and that is why I love it. The future is serious. The future is not a game. The future is not a gamble. The future is a serious now. I control my future. Jah gave me that guarantee. Strong I Am.

EPILOGUE

Anyone can help to make the world a better place. You don't have to be rich. You don't have to be poor. Anyone can help to make the world a better place. All that is required is to focus your attention on what is happening inside of your mind and your heart. Each person has a talent. A talent is a gift from the earth. It is also a blessing whenever it is used for the betterment of man. The more you get to know your talent, the more you get to know you on the inside. Then you will shine your light so bright, it will help to make the world a better place.